WHO IN THE WORLD WAS THE SECRETIVE PRINTER?

THE STORY OF JOHANNES GUTENBERG

by Robert Beckham
Illustrations by Jed Mickle

 **Peace Hill Press**

Charles City, VA

Books for the Well-Trained Mind

Publisher's Cataloging-in-Publication Data
(Provided by Quality Books, Inc.)

Beckham, Robert.
Who in the world was the secretive printer? : the story of
Johannes Gutenberg / by Robert Beckham ; illustrated by Jed Mickle.
p. cm.
Includes index.

SUMMARY:

The story of Johannes Gutenberg from his boyhood
to his development of movable type and the printing
press in Germany in the early 15th century.

Audience: Ages 5-12.

LCCN 2004112540
ISBN 0-9728603-6-3

1. Gutenberg, Johann, 1397?–1468 — Juvenile literature.
2. Printers — Germany — Biography — Juvenile literature.
3. Printing — History — Origin and antecedents — Juvenile literature.
[1. Gutenberg, Johann, 1397?–1468.
2. Printers.
3. Printing — History.]
I. Mickle, Jed.
II. Title.

Z126.Z7B43 2005   686.2'092
QBI04-800106

This *Who in the World* reader complements *The Story of the World, Vol. 2: The Middle Ages* (ISBN 0-9714129-3-6), also published by Peace Hill Press.

Peace Hill Press is an independent publisher creating high-quality educational books. Our award-winning resources—in history, reading, and grammar—are used by parents, teachers, libraries, and schools that want their students to be passionate about learning. For more about us, please visit our website, www.peacehillpress.com.

Table of Contents

CHAPTER 1

GROWING UP IN MAINZ

About six hundred years ago in the times of knights and castles, a baby boy was born in the town of Mainz, in the country of Germany. His parents named him Johannes.

If you were walking through Mainz on the day Johannes was born, you would see the Rhine River flowing on the other side of town. Boats float by, carrying travelers, and perhaps loads of cloth and other supplies to be sold in the city.

A strong wall stands around Mainz. People go in and out through four gates. There are towers at each gate where guards stand watch. The wall was built to help the people defend themselves when they are attacked by their enemies.

Inside the city, the steeple of a beautiful church rises high in the air. You may hear bells ringing. The main streets are paved with wood planks. Smaller streets are only mud. All the streets are crowded and noisy with people. You must watch out for the farm animals, too! Horses, cows, pigs, and sheep share the streets with the people. As you can imagine, the smell is pretty bad.

Along these crowded streets, you would find shops and inns. But you would not find libraries or bookstores in Mainz. One small bookstore now has more books than all the books in Germany when Johannes was a boy. That is because each copy of a book had to be written by hand. People called scribes would take a book that had already been written, and copy the words into another book. The scribes worked carefully, but of course, they sometimes made mistakes. So the copied books would have errors in them. And books took many weeks or months to copy!

Most of the books were owned by the Church leaders, with their Bibles and prayer books. Very rich people also owned a few books.

Johannes' family was among the rich people of Mainz. Johannes' father owned a big house and also a farm near the town. He received these things from his parents after they died. Johannes' family was honored and respected. His father was a leader in the town. They were known as an Old Family.

All the streets are crowded and noisy with people.

Johannes' father was an Old Family man because his parents were an Old Family. He did not have to do anything to become Old Family. He received special privileges and favors because of who his parents were.

Some of the special favors helped Johannes' father to earn money. He sold cloth for making clothes, and he was given a share of the profits from coin-making at the Mint (a place where money is made). Only Old Family people were allowed to do these things.

The honor of belonging to an Old Family was passed from parents to their children. So Johannes expected to be an Old Family man when he grew up. He too would receive special favors. Because his family was important, Johannes had a last name.

His last name, Gutenberg, came from the name of the house where his family lived. You see, most German people in 1400 did not have a last name. Only people who owned land and large houses and had money had last names. These last names were often taken from the name of the house where the family lived. So when Johannes' family came to live in the Gutenberg house, Gutenberg became their last name.

Johannes had a last name and special favors. He also got to go to school. But in his school, Johannes had very few books. One book helped him learn to read and write Latin. Latin was the language of the Romans, who had once

Johannes had very few books.

ruled over people in many lands—people who spoke many languages. These people used Latin to speak with each other.

By the time Johannes was born, the Romans did not rule anything, and nobody spoke Latin in their everyday activities. So why did Johannes learn Latin? Because all educated, Christian people were taught Latin. Latin became the special language of the Christian Church. Just like the Roman Empire, the Christian Church spread to many lands where people spoke many languages. The leaders of the Church could talk and write to each other in Latin. Even the Bibles that they used were written in Latin.

Johannes also learned simple arithmetic. He was probably taught arithmetic using the same kind of numbers—0, 1, 2, 3, 4, 5, 6, 7, 8, and 9—that you learn today. These numbers were first invented in India. Then, Arab people learned them. Finally, knowledge of the new numbers spread to Johannes' country. The new numbers made arithmetic much easier. Many German people still did arithmetic with Roman Numerals that looked like letters of the alphabet: I, V, L, C, M. Even easy adding or subtracting was very hard to do with Roman Numerals.

*The leaders of the Church could talk
and write to each other in Latin.*

CHAPTER 2

WORKING AT THE MINT

When Johannes was a young man, in 1419, his father died. Johannes expected to be an Old Family man, just as his father was. But that did not happen. His mother did not belong to an Old Family before she married. So the other Old Families in Mainz decided that she and her three children could no longer be an Old Family. They lost some of their special privileges.

But Johannes' mother still had a lot of money and two houses. His older brother moved into the big house. Johannes didn't move into either house because he already had his own place to live. But he still depended on his father for money. Johannes got a small amount of money after his father died, but it was not enough to live on. He needed to find a job.

Johannes got a job at the Mint, where coins were made.

Johannes got a job at the Mint, where coins were made. The Mint was close to the house where he grew up. As a boy, he watched the men making coins, and admired their skill.

Look at the words and figures on a coin. You can read on the coin "United States of America" and "In God We Trust." Perhaps a man's head or an eagle is stamped on the coin. Words and figures were also stamped on coins when Johannes worked at the Mint, but the coins were harder to make. Someone first had to carve the words and figures on a small piece of metal, to make a stamp. Then, the stamp would be pressed down onto the coin. Craftsmen carved the stamps with small, very sharp knives. This was the hardest job at the Mint, but Johannes learned how to do it.

Johannes had a pretty good job as a craftsman at the Mint, but he could not hope to advance to a better job. All the best jobs were reserved for members of the Old Families, and Johannes was no longer an Old Family man. Also, Mainz was not a very happy place to be. The rich Old Families and the skilled workers like Johannes argued and quarreled constantly. Who should pay taxes? Who should receive special favors? Who should pick the city's leaders? They could not agree on anything.

After his father died, Johannes spent about ten more years in Mainz. He did not have a wife or even a girlfriend. Johannes was close to thirty years old, and he had lived

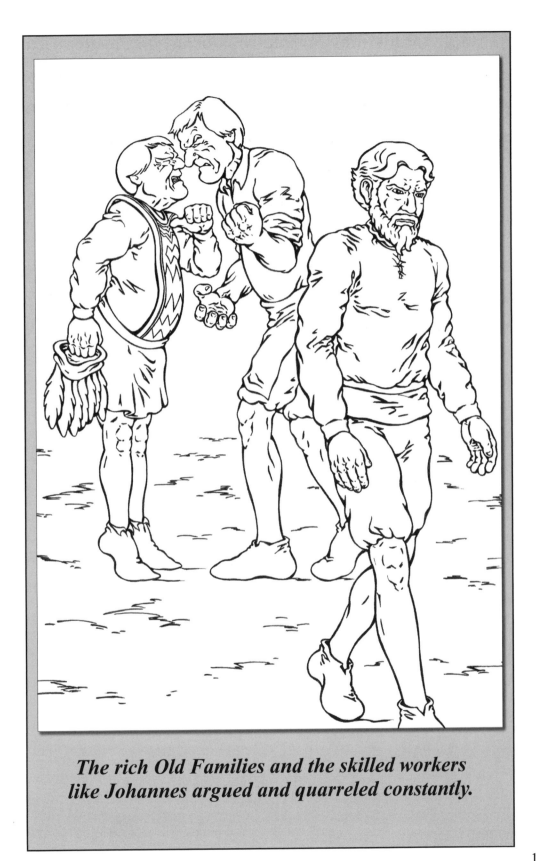

The rich Old Families and the skilled workers like Johannes argued and quarreled constantly.

in Mainz all his life. Now he was bored and restless. He decided it was time to leave Mainz and try to find a better place to live. He moved to the city of Strasbourg, which was a two-day boat trip up the Rhine River from Mainz.

About the same time, his mother died. Her money and two houses were divided among her three children. Johannes received a large amount of money, so he did not have to get a job right away. He moved to a tiny village just outside Strasbourg. There, with not many people around, he started doing something in secret.

CHAPTER 3

A Secret Project

The only thing his neighbors knew was that he had a small shop where he worked with gold and other metals. Perhaps he made gold jewelry. But he was doing something else, too, that he did not talk about. Even today, we are not sure what he was doing. We think he was already trying to build a machine that would print books. Why do you suppose he kept it secret? Most likely, he was afraid someone would steal his work.

When Johannes started building a printing machine, he already knew a lot about how to make letters of the alphabet out of small pieces of metal. He had learned this skill when he made coins at the Mint. Now he used his knowledge to make metal letters. These letters, made out of metal, are called "type." One letter is one piece of type. Johannes thought that he could put pieces of type together, to make a word—just like you might make words out of magnetic letters on your refrigerator. Then if he spread ink on the type and pressed it against a piece of paper, the word would be stamped on the paper. The type could stamp out the same word again and again, much faster than a scribe could write by hand.

Johannes was just beginning a very hard task. He could easily make a few pieces of type, but he would need several thousand pieces to print a book. He also needed a good way to press a whole page of type against a piece of paper. Finally, he needed to find the kinds of paper and ink that would work best on his press. Years of hard work lay ahead of him.

By now, Johannes was about thirty-five years old. He had money and a good reputation, and plenty of girls wanted to marry him. Johannes spent a lot of time with one girl named Annie.

Soon, Annie's mother began to tell all her friends and neighbors that Annie was going to marry Johannes. But although Johannes like Annie, he did not want to get married. He worked long hours in his shop. The rest of the time, he was probably thinking about his work. He had become very excited about his secret project. He did not have time for anything else—even for Annie.

Annie's mother became very upset. She accused
Johannes of breaking his promise to marry Annie.

Annie's mother became very upset. She accused Johannes of breaking his promise to marry Annie. She found a man, Mr. Schott, who would be a witness for her. Mr. Schott claimed he had heard Johannes promise to marry Annie. Then, Annie's mother asked a Church court to order Johannes to marry her daughter.

Mr. Schott told the court judges that he heard Johannes promise to marry Annie. Johannes was angry. He told the court judges that he never promised to marry Annie. He called Mr. Schott a cheat and a liar. Then it was Mr. Schott's turn to get mad. The judges agreed that Johannes should not have insulted Mr. Schott in public, and made Johannes pay a small fine. But the judges also agreed that Johannes did not break a promise to Annie. There was no marriage. Johannes never did get married!

Soon Johannes faced a new problem. He needed lots of money to carry on his secret project. He told a few people about what he was doing, and three men gave Johannes money to help complete his project. Then they would share in the profits and make a lot of money themselves. At least, that is what they thought.

CHAPTER 4

THOUSANDS OF SMALL MIRRORS

Johannes worked hard, but his printing press was far from complete. It would be years before he could expect to earn money from printing books. The three men worried that Johannes would never be able to repay them. So Johannes thought of something he could make and sell quickly to earn money. He decided to make mirrors, thousands of small mirrors. Mirrors were often made from polished metal at that time. Johannes worked with metal, so mirrors would be easy for him to make. More importantly, he knew just who would buy his mirrors—the common people of Germany.

Some of the things they did sound foolish to us. Here's the story of why these people wanted mirrors:

A great king named Charlemagne ruled the land long before Johannes was born. After he died, his body was placed in a golden casket. The casket was not buried. It was placed in a cathedral. Many people came to the cathedral to see the golden casket of the great king. Soon, other objects like a woman's robe and baby clothes were displayed beside the casket. The people were told that the clothes belonged to the baby Jesus, and Jesus' mother Mary had worn the robe. This was not true, but the people believed it.

Many people came to the cathedral to see the golden casket and touch the holy clothes. They believed these things had magical healing powers. Soon, the crowds became so great that they could not all get inside the cathedral. The leaders decided that the holy objects would only be displayed for two weeks, every seven years. During that time, the objects were moved outside of the cathedral, onto a wooden stage. That way, great crowds could see the holy things, even though they could not get close enough to touch them.

The people believed that the healing power could not work if they did not touch the holy objects. But someone suggested another way to receive the magic. If a person stood in the crowd and held a small mirror overhead, then the healing energy would flow into the mirror. Everyone could go home happy, thinking they had mirrors that contained magical healing powers. This may sound foolish to us. But the people who believed it had hard lives. When they got

The people believed that if a person held a small mirror overhead, then the healing energy would flow into it.

sick, there were few medicines and few doctors who knew how to cure them. They were willing to try almost anything to get help for their troubles.

Johannes knew when the holy objects would be displayed again. He planned to have his mirrors ready for sale. Then something terrible happened. The holy objects were not displayed that year because an awful disease spread over Germany, causing sickness and death.

The disease was bubonic plague. The people called it the Black Death. The Black Death came from fleas on rats. It can be cured now, but then, nobody knew what caused it. So of course, there was no cure. Millions of people died when the Black Death struck. Whole towns were sometimes wiped out.

When the Black Death started, people were afraid to travel to see the holy objects. They were afraid that if they traveled to other places in Germany, they might catch the plague. The church leaders knew that people would not travel, so they decided to delay the display of the holy objects until the plague was over. Since there was no display to go to, people did not need to buy mirrors. Johannes had already made many mirrors to sell. Now nobody wanted to buy them. He did not earn any money from his mirrors!

The three men who had invested their money with Johannes were more worried than ever that they would lose their money. Then one of the men died. His family was very

They took Johannes to court, and asked the judge to make Johannes pay back the money.

upset when they learned about the money he had loaned to Johannes. They took Johannes to court, and asked the judge to make Johannes pay back the money.

The judge listened to the family's story. The two brothers of the dead man complained that their dead brother had given a great deal of money to Johannes and received nothing in return. Then Johannes told his side of the story. He talked about his bad luck with the mirrors that could not be sold. He explained that he was making something special, and that the money was spent on his special project. The mysterious project wasn't complete yet. He needed more time!

The judge decided that Johannes had not done anything dishonest. The lost money was not his fault. He did not have to repay anything.

CHAPTER 5

THREE MORE TASKS

When Johannes returned to his shop, he looked around at the pieces of his mysterious project—the printing press. He had at least three tasks left.

1. He had to make the type—letters of the alphabet made out of metal. This was probably the hardest job Johannes had to do. The tiny metal letters had to be perfectly shaped, exactly the same thickness, and perfectly flat. Each piece of type had to be just right, and Johannes needed several thousand pieces! He had to find a way to make them quickly. Johannes truly showed his creative genius in solving the problem of making type. He invented a tool called a hand-held mold. The tool was very difficult to

make, but easy to use. He heated metal until it melted, and poured it into his hand-held mold. When the metal cooled and hardened, he had a piece of type, a letter of the alphabet shaped in metal. Other metalworkers knew how to use molds to shape metal. But they were slow and clumsy. Johannes' hand-held mold tool allowed him to make type quickly, easily, the same every time.

2. He needed paper and ink. People already knew how to make paper and ink, but Johannes spent years trying to make just the right kind of paper and ink for his printing press.

3. He needed a press. Imagine that his press looked something like two table tops that could be tightly pressed together. One table top had some frames on it to hold a few pages of paper in place. The other table top had frames to hold the type in place. Johannes would arrange his pieces of type to form all the words on a page of the book he wanted to print. He formed a page of type for every page of paper on his press. Then he rubbed ink on his type and tightly pressed the pages of type against the pages of paper. When he opened his press, he saw nice printed pages of paper.

When Johannes finished printing the pages in his press, he only had to put more paper in the press to make another copy of the same pages. He could make many copies in a short time.

**When he opened his press,
he saw nice printed pages of paper.**

But his press could only hold a few pages, not all the pages in a book. Now comes the most wonderful part of Johannes' invention! When he finished making copies of the pages in his press, he simply moved the type out of the frames and arranged the type into new words on new pages. He was ready to print some more pages. It was quick and easy. No one ever before had figured out how to do this. We call it <u>printing with movable type</u>.

By now, Johannes was about forty years old. Johannes earned money from the gold jewelry and ornaments he made in his metal shop, but he still had not printed anything on his press. War came to Strasbourg in 1444, making it a dangerous place to live. The time had come for Johannes to move on.

He simply moved the type out of the frames
and arranged the type into new words on new pages.

CHAPTER 6

A WORK OF ART

We do not know where Johannes lived for the next four years. But in 1448, he was back in Mainz. By that time, he was finally ready to do some printing on his press. What would he print? The Bible was his first choice. The church leaders needed Bibles. They had the money to pay for nice Bibles. However, the Bible would be a very big printing job. Also, the church leaders would not be satisfied with plain printing. They would expect Johannes' Bibles to be as beautiful as the Bibles copied by the scribes.

Johannes needed some small jobs to practice on. He printed a little school book that students used to learn Latin. The book was just a few pages and easy to print. Even better, he earned money by selling the little book. Some of the city leaders liked his work, and gave him other small printing jobs to do.

After he had practiced on the small jobs, Johannes started printing the Bible in 1452. He finished printing it about two years later, in the fall of 1454. One hundred and eighty copies of the Bible, written in Latin, came from Johannes' printing presses. Each copy had 1,275 pages. During that time, he had two print shops, and he hired between twenty and thirty people to help him.

Johannes wanted his Bibles to be beautiful and to be printed perfectly. And he was successful. The letters of his Bibles were shaped in fancy curves and scrolls. Johannes used red and blue ink as well as black ink, to add color to his books. The borders of the pages were decorated with curves and scrolls like lace. Johannes' Bibles were works of art.

But Johannes' success in creating beautiful Bibles came at a great price. He spent all the money he had and all the money he could borrow to complete the Bibles. Most of the money he borrowed came from a man named Mr. Fust. Like Johannes' three partners of earlier years, Mr. Fust worried that he would lose his money.

Several months passed. Mr. Fust still had not been paid. Rulers and church leaders, even from far away, had seen or heard about Johannes' Bibles. They placed their orders, and soon Johannes had an order for every Bible. It looked like

Back in Mainz, Johannes began printing Bibles in 1452.

Johannes would be able to pay all his debts and have money left for himself.

But although Johannes had orders for the Bibles, he had not yet received any money for them. Before Johannes had received any money, Mr. Fust went before a judge and demanded that Johannes pay his debt without delay. Since Johannes had no money, Mr. Fust asked the judge to make Johannes give him one of the print shops and all the Bibles.

Johannes could have appeared before the judge. He could have explained how he could not pay Mr. Fust at the moment, but he soon would be able to pay him. The judge might have given Johannes a little more time until he could receive payment for the Bibles. Then there would be enough money for everyone.

But when the time came for Johannes' last chance to speak to the judge and defend himself, he did not even go to see the judge. He only asked a couple of friends to go to the court and hear what the judge decided. Without Johannes to give his side of the story, the judge had no choice but to agree with Mr. Fust. One of Johannes' shops, the printing presses in the shop, and the Bibles were all given to Mr. Fust.

One of Johannes' shops, the printing presses in the shop, and the Bibles were all given to Mr. Fust.

Johannes' invention was beginning to change the way that books were made—a change that would last forever.

CHAPTER 7

THE GIFT OF JOHANNES GUTENBERG

We can only guess why Johannes did not try harder to keep his shop and Bibles. Maybe he was just tired of working so hard. Johannes had used his time, energy, and all the money he could find to print the Bibles. That is all he cared about.

Mr. Fust was now the new owner of a print shop. He did not know anything about printing, but he was smart. He hired Johannes' best helper to run his shop. They did very well. All the Bibles were sold, and other very fine printing work was done. Johannes had created the printing press and printed the Bibles, but he did not receive a penny from the sale of the Bibles.

You can imagine how sad and disappointed Johannes must have felt. He continued to live in Mainz for a time, and do small printing jobs himself. Then another war, with more fighting, came to Mainz, and Johannes moved out to the village where his family had once owned a farm. Once again, he took his printing press with him and kept working.

Now Mr. Fust had a printing shop and Johannes also had a printing shop. Other men who had learned printing from Johannes started printing shops of their own. Printing shops started to spread throughout the country. Johannes' invention was beginning to change the way that books were made—a change that would last forever.

Late in his life, Johannes finally received some of the honor that was due him. Adolf, the ruler of the area around Mainz, knew the great work that Johannes had done. He rewarded Johannes with clothing, food, and wine every year for the rest of his life.

Johannes died February 3, 1468, and was buried at St. Francis' Church in Mainz. In the next few years, other printers built many more printing presses. All over Germany, and in all the countries around Germany, millions of books were printed. People read and wrote more and more books about history, science, and art. Johannes' invention, the printing press, gave people a way to learn about their world and share their knowledge.

Gutenberg Bibles are owned by universities and museums, and kept in glass cases, where they are carefully protected.

Today, only about fifty of Johannes' Bibles remain. They are called Gutenberg Bibles, in honor of Johannes. You cannot afford to buy one. They cost millions of dollars. Gutenberg Bibles are owned by universities and museums, and kept in glass cases, where they are carefully protected.

But thanks to Johannes Gutenberg, the world is filled with many books that you can touch, read, and take home—like this one. That is the gift of Johannes Gutenberg.

*Thanks to Johannes Gutenberg,
the world is filled with many books
that you can touch, read, and take home.*

INDEX

Gutenberg, Johannes. *See* Johannes.

Johannes
    Attended school 4-6, *5*
    Began making a printing machine 14
    Began printing the Bible 29
    Decided to leave Mainz 12
    Died and was recognized for work 36
    From an Old Family 2, 4, 8
    Got a job at the Mint *9,* 10
    Learned arithmetic 6
    Learned Latin 4
    Planned to sell mirrors 20
    Went to court 16, *21,* 22

Machine, printing 13 *see also Printing Press*

Mainz 10, 31
    Johannes left 12
    Johannes returned to 29
    Life inside of 1-2, *3*
    Old Families in 8
    Saint Francis' church in 36

Mint 4, 8, *9,* 10, 13

Mirrors 17-22, *19*

Mold, hand-held
    Johannes invented 23
    Used to make type 24

Old Families
    Privileges of 4
    Quarreled with skilled workers *11*

Press, printing 15, 17, 23, 24, *25,* 26, 29, 30, 32, 33
    Johannes created 35
    Printers built many 36

Rhine River 1, 12

Schott, Mr. 16

Scribes 2, 14, 29

Strasbourg
  Johannes moved from 26
  Johannes moved to 12

Type 14, *27*
  Johannes learned how to make 23-26
  Movable 26

ALSO AVAILABLE FROM PEACE HILL PRESS:

Who in the World Was the UNREADY KING?
THE STORY OF ETHELRED

by Connie Clark
illustrations by Jed Mickle

Ethelred's mother stood behind him. The archbishop smeared holy oil on Ethelred's shoulders and hands. He gave Ethelred a heavy sword and placed a gold crown on his head. The crown was too big—it fell over his eyes, and Ethelred almost dropped the sword on the archbishop's foot. **How did Ethelred become king when he was only ten years old?**

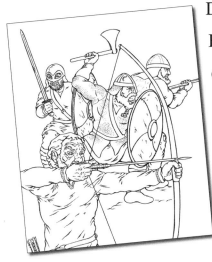

Discover the intriguing story of Ethelred, England's last Anglo-Saxon king. In this engaging biography, Connie Clark tells the tale of the boy king who handed England over to the Vikings. How did Ethelred and his sons lose their country to the northern invaders? Find out, with *Who in the World Was the Unready King? The Story of Ethelred*.